Confirmation Preparation for Young People

Alive in the Spirit!

Family Book

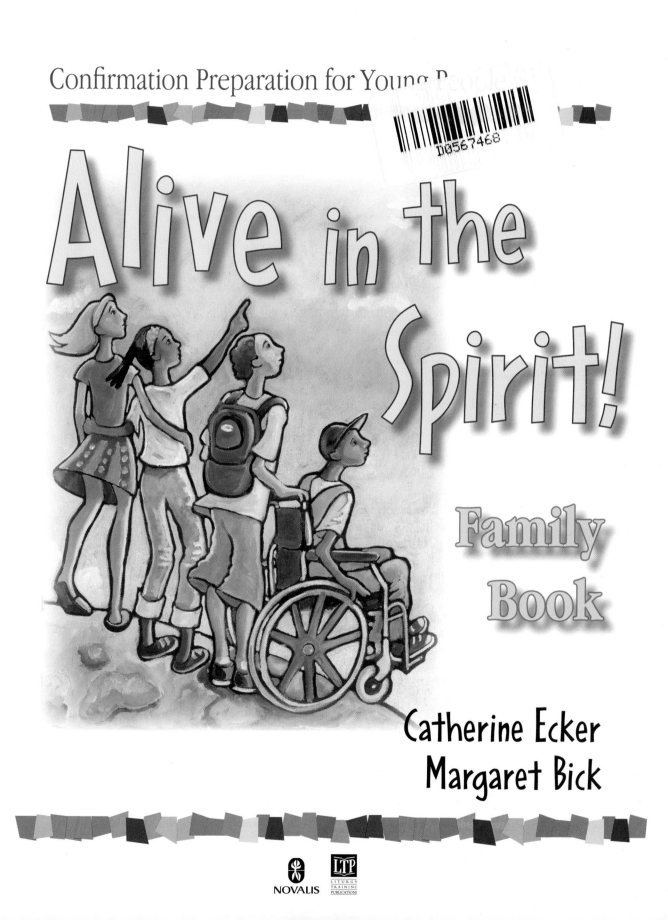

Catherine Ecker

Margaret Bick

NOVALIS

LTP
LITURGY
TRAINING
PUBLICATIONS

NOVALIS

LITURGY
TRAINING
PUBLICATIONS

Editor: Patrick Gallagher
Cover: Anna Payne-Krzyzanowski
Layout: Anna Payne-Krzyzanowski
Photo credits: Bill Wittman: pp. 19, 30, 31, 34;
CP: p. 25 (CP 3529842)

Publishing Office
10 Lower Spadina Avenue, Suite 400
Toronto, Ontario, Canada
Canada M5V 2Z2

Head Office
4475 Frontenac Street
Montréal, Québec,
H2H 2S2

www.novalis.ca

We acknowledge the financial support of the Government of Canada through the Canada Book Fund for business development activities.

ISBN: 978-2-89507-609-4 (Novalis)
Printed in Canada.

Reprint 2010

To my children, Jake and Nicole.

—*C.E.*

Nihil Obstat
Reverend Louis J. Cameli, S.T.D.
Censor Deputatus
January 4, 2006

Imprimatur
Bishop-elect George J. Rassas
Vicar General
Archdiocese of Chicago
January 11, 2006

*The **Nihil Obstat** and **Imprimatur** are official declarations that a book is free of doctrinal and moral error. No implication is contained therein that those who have granted the **Nihil Obstat** and **Imprimatur** agree with the content, opinions, or statements expressed. Nor do they assume any legal responsibility associated with publication.*

Published in the United Stated of America by Liturgy Training Publications,
1800 North Hermitage Avenue,
Chicago IL 60622-1101;
1-800-933-1800,
fax 1-800-933-7094,
email orders@ltp.org.
See our website at www.ltp.org.

Alive in the Spirit!: Confirmation Preparation for Young People, Family Book
ISBN 10: 1-56854-603-3 (Liturgy Training Publications)
ISBN 13: 978-1-56854-603-2 (Liturgy Training Publications)
AISCPF

Acknowledgments

We would very much like to thank the following reviewers for their valuable contribution to the development of this program: Char Deslippe, Religious Education Coordinator, Diocese of Victoria, BC • Sr. Mary-Ann Bates, Diocesan Director of Catechetics, Diocese of Prince George, BC • Sr. Gertrude Mulholland, Our Lady of Perpetual Help Parish, Sherwood Park, AB • Susan Suttie, Religious Education Consultant, Diocese of Calgary, AB • Sr. Lorraine Couture, Catechetics Coordinator, Rural Catechetics Office, Prince Albert, SK • Agnes Rolheiser, Rural Catechetics, Diocese of Saskatoon, SK • Carol Anne Seed, Director of Catechetics and Faith Formation, Archdiocese of Winnipeg, MB • Fr. Murray Kroetsch, Saint Pius X Church, Brantford, ON • Emily Di Fruscia, Assistant Director, Archdiocesan Office for Faith Formation, Montreal, QC • Paul Toner, Director of Liturgy, Archdiocese of Moncton, Dieppe, NB • Madelyn Ramier, Diocesan Director of Catechetics, Diocese of Saint John, Fredericton, NB • Marilyn Sweet, Director of Programs, Archdiocese of Halifax, NS • Margaret Craddock, Archdiocesan Director of Catechesis, Archdiocese of St. John's, NL.

5 4 3   14 13 12 11 10

Table of Contents

Welcome to Alive in the Spirit!

It is a privilege to be part of your preparation for the celebration of confirmation.

Some time ago you celebrated the sacrament of baptism, which marked the beginning of your journey in the Christian community. Although you may not recall your baptism, this program will be an opportunity to celebrate and recall the actions and rituals surrounding baptism. This recollection will help you learn more about what is involved in living as a confirmed disciple.

It has been an adventure to write this book for you. For each session you will find suggestions for activities. You need not complete all of them – just choose the ones that are most suitable. We have also included some prayers for your family prayer time. You will see that what happens in baptism and confirmation prepares us and leads us to celebrate Sunday eucharist.

We hope this book provides you with an opportunity to deepen your parish connection.

May you and your family discover the wonder and joy of living as disciples.

Catherine and Margaret

Session 1

Baptized with Water

Dear family,

Because baptism, confirmation and eucharist are linked as sacraments of initiation, preparing for confirmation begins with recalling our baptism.

As part of our first gathering, we created a ritual celebration to recall the water used in baptism. We thanked God for the gift of water in our lives and discovered why we use water in baptism.

Family involvement is an important part of confirmation preparation. You can be part of your child's confirmation in a number of ways. You are invited to:

* share photographs or other memories of your child's baptism
* be sure to include your child's godparents in the confirmation (this is a good time to plan a visit or send a letter)
* work with your child to complete pages 9, 10 and 11
* share your memories of and information about your own baptism on page 9
* plan a family meal during the coming week
* say together the prayers on pages 12 and 13
* gather on Sunday with the parish community for eucharist.

We look forward to our next session on _____ at _____.

Thank you.

Catechist

Water in Church

Each time we Christians enter a church, dip our hand in the holy water font, and trace with water the sign of the cross on ourselves, we are recalling our baptism. This simple gesture reminds us that God has created us anew through baptism. We may not actually remember our baptism when we cross ourselves, but this action helps us recall that we are disciples of Jesus and members of God's family.

As baptized disciples, we also prepare and celebrate our confirmation. These two sacraments are so closely linked that preparing for confirmation means first recalling our baptism. And baptism and confirmation prepare us for eucharist, for celebrating at the table of the Lord.

Baptism, Confirmation and Eucharist

When adults or older children prepare for initiation in the Catholic Church they spend a lot of time, sometimes years, preparing themselves. At the end of this time, the Church celebrates with them the three sacraments of initiation: baptism, confirmation and eucharist.

When we are baptized as babies or young children we often celebrate confirmation after we have begun sharing in communion. To share in communion is to share in the body and blood of Christ under the form of bread and wine.

On the day of your baptism you began your faith journey. Your family has been a part of your journey and it continues each week as you gather for the parish celebration of Sunday eucharist. Confirmation prepares us to celebrate eucharist in a richer or deeper way.

My Baptism Story

My Name ....

Where I was baptized ....

Date of Baptism ....

Godparents ....

Special Memories ....

....

....

My Name ....

Where I was baptized ....

Date of Baptism ....

Godparents ....

Special Memories ....

....

Renewing Our Promises

Every year at Easter we are invited to renew our baptismal promises. On the day of their confirmation, candidates are asked to renew their baptismal promises again.

We begin this renewal by first renouncing sin and then professing our faith. Our answer to the questions is a strong I DO!

Together fill in the blanks. (You can look at the Word Bank on page 11.)

Renunciation of Sin

Do you _____ Satan?

And all _____ works?

And all his _____ _____?

Profession of Faith

Do you _____ in God, the _____ almighty,

creator of _____ and earth?

Do you believe in _____ _____,

his only Son our Lord, who was _____ of the Virgin

Mary, was _____ , _____ and was

buried, rose from the _____ , and is now _____

at the right hand of the _____?

Do you believe in the Holy _____,

the holy Catholic Church, the _____ of saints,

the forgiveness of _____ and life _____?

⁓⁓⁓ Word Bank ⁓⁓⁓

everlasting	Christ	born	reject
seated	heaven	dead	his
empty	believe	sins	father
Jesus	died	communion	Spirit
father	crucified	promises	

When we renew our baptismal promises we are reminded of how we are to live.

What do you think it means to reject Satan?

....

....

What do you think life everlasting may be like?

....

....

The Lord's Prayer

Our Father,
who art in heaven,
hallowed be thy name;
thy kingdom come;
thy will be done
on earth as it is in heaven.
Give us this day our daily bread;
and forgive us our trespasses
as we forgive those who trespass against us;
and lead us not into temptation,
but deliver us from evil.

Amen.

Confirmation Prayer

Loving God,
We come to know something of your greatness
through the gifts of sight, sound, touch,
smell and taste.

Help us to grow in understanding
the love you have for us
and guide us to live as members of your family
so that all people will be led to you.

We ask this prayer in the name of Jesus,
your Son,
by the power of the Holy Spirit.
Amen.

Session 2

Anointed with Oil

Dear family,

As part of our gathering we recalled why oil is used during baptism. We discovered how anointing with oil helps us understand our role as baptized followers of Jesus and as members of God's family.

Your involvement in confirmation preparation is important. You are invited to

- share a family meal together at least once each week
- remember in prayer all those preparing to celebrate confirmation
- read with your child pages 16, 17 and 18
- read page 19 together and encourage your child to contact her or his sponsor
- complete page 20 together
- pray together Psalm 23 and the Confirmation Prayer on pages 21 and 22
- continue to gather on Sunday with the parish community for eucharist.

We look forward to our next session on _____ at _____.

All the candidates have been asked to wear a special piece of clothing to our next session. The clothing could be special for any reason: it could be a favourite item; a "lucky sweater" worn at sports events; a favourite colour or texture; or a gift from someone.

Thank you.

Catechist

Oil in Church

The Church uses three sacred oils: the oil of the sick, the oil of catechumens, and chrism (KRIZ-um). The oil of the sick is used to comfort, strengthen and heal when we are sick. The oil of catechumens is used to strengthen catechumens on their journey of faith.

The perfumed oil of chrism (KRIZ-um) is used in four different anointings:
* when a baby is baptized
* when we are confirmed
* when priests receive holy orders
* when a church building and altar are dedicated.

All these different uses of chrism deepen our identity with Christ.

My Life in the Christian Community

On the feast of Christ the King, just before Advent begins, the Church prays:

".... You anointed Jesus Christ, your only Son, with the oil of gladness, as the eternal high priest and universal king...that he may present to you, his almighty Father, an eternal and universal kingdom: a kingdom of truth and life, a kingdom of holiness and grace, a kingdom of justice, love and peace...."

As disciples we are expected to work so that the kingdom of God may flourish. We are able to work for truth, justice and peace when we co-operate in our lives with the Spirit of God.

Co-operating with God's Spirit

How do we learn to co-operate with the Spirit of God? The first thing we have to do is learn how to listen to God. This can be tricky. We live in a busy and noisy world. It's possible to wake up to the sounds of a radio, to be surrounded by conversations, television and music all day, and to fall asleep to a favourite CD. These constant sounds can make it difficult to hear God.

During the coming weeks, set some time aside, even only five minutes each day, and simply listen to God. Here's what you can do.

Turn off all outside noise and ... just listen. At first this might seem difficult or a little unusual. Begin by sitting comfortably and telling God that you are ready to listen. Sometimes it helps to repeat a phrase over and over. You can try "Jesus is Lord."

Give it a chance. You'll be surprised at how easy it can be to listen to God.

Your Sponsor

During the celebration of confirmation the bishop or priest will anoint your head with chrism. (Sometimes the bishop may give permission to the priest to confirm.) He will say your name and then these words: "Be sealed with the Gift of the Holy Spirit." You will answer, "Amen."

The Church prays that the newly confirmed will be attentive to the presence of the Holy Spirit in their lives. Your sponsor will support and guide you in discovering how to live as a disciple.

During the coming week, telephone or write a note to your sponsor and share one or two things you have discovered about baptism and confirmation.

Working for the Kingdom of God

We are called to work together so that the kingdom of God may flourish. We do this because it is the way Jesus calls us to live.

Name two ways that you can work with your family for the kingdom of God. Record your ideas below.

1. ....

....

....

2. ....

....

....

....

(Hint: Think of ways you support and care for others in your family and community.)

Psalm 23

The Lord is my shepherd,
I shall not want.
He makes me lie down in green pastures;
he leads me beside still waters;
he restores my soul.
He leads me in right paths
for his name's sake.

Even though I walk through the darkest valley,
I fear no evil;
for you are with me;
your rod and your staff—
they comfort me.

You prepare a table before me
in the presence of my enemies;
you anoint my head with oil;
my cup overflows.
Surely goodness and mercy shall follow me
   all the days of my life,
and I shall dwell in the house of the Lord
   my whole life long.

Confirmation Prayer

Loving God,
through anointing with oil
we come to know something of your love for us.

Help us to grow in wisdom and courage,
guiding us to walk as your disciples
ready to love one another.

We ask this prayer in the name of Jesus,
your Son,
by the power of the Holy Spirit.

Amen.

Session 3

Clothed in Christ

Dear family,

At baptism the Church proclaims: "You have become a new creation and clothed yourself in Christ." St. Paul reminds us that through baptism we have been joined to Christ forever. We have a new identity.

At our gathering, we recalled that marking ourselves with the sign of the cross reminds us of our new Christian identity.

Your participation in confirmation preparation is important. You are invited to

- ✳ trace the sign of the cross on your child's forehead at least once during the day (before school, before bed, or after your child has fallen asleep are all appropriate moments)
- ✳ plan a family meal together
- ✳ begin each meal with the sign of the cross and a prayer of thanksgiving
- ✳ read together and complete pages 25 to 28
- ✳ pray together the Prayer of St. Francis and the Confirmation Prayer on pages 30 and 31
- ✳ prepare invitations together for those you would like to attend the confirmation celebration
- ✳ continue to gather on Sunday with the parish community for eucharist.

We look forward to our next session on _____ at _____.

Please send your child's baptismal candle (or a 10 inch taper) to the next session.

Thank you.

Catechist

The Cross

In 1984 Pope John Paul II gave the youth of the world a large wooden cross to remind them of their role as Christians and followers of Jesus. He told them, "My dear young people ... I entrust to you the sign of... the Cross of Christ! Carry it throughout the world as a symbol of Christ's love for humanity, and announce to everyone that only in the death and resurrection of Christ can we find salvation and redemption."

The cross is a visible reminder of our new identity. Each time we trace the cross on our body we recall that through the waters of baptism we have been given a new identity.

When we gather for eucharist we trace the cross on ourselves more than once. When we trace the cross on our forehead or body we say, "In the name of the Father, and of the Son, and of the Holy Spirit." *Why do we say these words?*

....

....

....

....

....

My Life in the Christian Community

In the gospels we read that Jesus was filled with the Spirit. At baptism we receive the Spirit. In confirmation the Church prays with us that we will be aware of the presence of the Holy Spirit in our lives. It is the strength of the Holy Spirit that helps us to be more like Christ.

The presence of the Holy Spirit is part of the mystery of our faith. Although we can't fully explain the actions of the Holy Spirit in our lives, Christians name seven gifts to describe how the Holy Spirit helps us. These gifts are

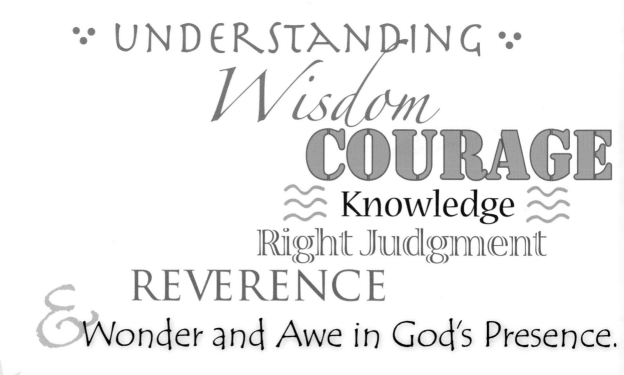

UNDERSTANDING

Wisdom

COURAGE

Knowledge

Right Judgment

REVERENCE

& Wonder and Awe in God's Presence.

The Gifts of the Holy Spirit

As Christians we pray for the Holy Spirit to guide us in our lives.

Choose two or three of the gifts of the Holy Spirit, and write down how you think each gift could be important in living as a disciple of Christ.

Gifts of the Holy Spirit

....

....

These Gifts are important because

....

....

....

....

....

Christian Symbols

Symbols are an important part of our Christian family heritage. Complete one of the following activities that use our Christian family symbols.

* Create a colourful centrepiece using water, oil and a cross. You can make the cross from wood, fabric, paper or other materials.

* Make placemats for your family table using pictures or images of water, oil and a cross.

The Communion of Saints

Just as symbols are part of our Christian family heritage, so too are people who have lived before us and worked to create the kingdom of God.

At Mass, we declare that we believe in the communion of saints. The communion of saints are Christian women and men who have lived and died and are now living in heaven. Think of the communion of saints as our heroes or as our cheering section. We often ask the saints to pray with and for us so that we may be stronger in our faith.

St. Francis of Assisi, whose feast day is October 4, is one of the best-known members of the communion of saints. His prayer for peace on the next page is a prayer that asks for God's help so that we can live as disciples.

Prayer of St. Francis

Lord, make me an instrument of your peace.
Where there is hatred, let me sow love;
where there is injury, pardon;
where there is doubt, faith;
where there is despair, hope;
where there is darkness, light;
and where there is sadness, joy.

Divine Master,
grant that I may not so much seek
to be consoled as to console,
to be understood as to understand,
to be loved as to love.

For it is in giving that we receive,
in pardoning that we are pardoned,
and in dying
that we are born to eternal life.

Confirmation Prayer

Loving God,
Through the waters of baptism
we were given a new identity,
united to Christ.

Help us to grow in right judgment and reverence,
guiding us to walk as your disciples
ready to love one another.
We ask this prayer in the name of Jesus,
your Son,
by the power of the Holy Spirit.

Amen.

Session 4

Enlightened

by Christ

Dear family,

At our last gathering we recalled that at baptism we receive a lit candle and are told that we have been enlightened by Christ and should always walk as children of light. We discussed what it means to walk as children of light and how we can be a light for others.

During these final weeks before confirmation your continued participation is important. You are invited to

* trace the sign of the cross on your child's forehead at the end of the day
* light the baptismal candle before each meal (if the baptismal candle has been used up, use the candle from our session)
* begin each meal with the sign of the cross and a prayer of thanksgiving
* remember in prayer all those preparing to celebrate confirmation
* together read and complete pages 34, 35 and 36
* join your child in praying the prayers on pages 37 and 38
* continue to gather on Sunday with the parish community for eucharist.

We look forward to our next session on _____ at _____.

Thank you.

Catechist

The Easter Candle

ach year after darkness has fallen on Holy Saturday, the Church lights a new fire, blesses the fire, and lights the Easter candle. The Easter candle burns brightly for the fifty days of Easter.

The Easter candle reminds us that Jesus has risen from the dead, destroying the darkness of death forever. The Easter candle burns during every celebration of baptism and the newly baptized receive a lit candle announcing that they have been enlightened by Christ and are to walk as children of the light.

The Light of Christ

Jesus calls himself the light of the world. He says,

**"I am the light of the world.
Whoever follows me will never walk in darkness
but will have the light of life."**

(John 8:12)

Where in your life

do you see

the light of Jesus?

Name two or three

people who shine the

light of Christ for you.

Sharing the Light

Jesus tells us,

> **"You are the light of the world.... No one after lighting a lamp puts it under the bushel basket, but on the lampstand and it gives light to all in the house."**

(Matthew 5:14-15)

Being a baptized and confirmed Christian includes sharing the light of Christ with others. Jesus invites our family to be a light for others. Decide together how your family gives light to others. Write down some of your ideas.

Glory to God

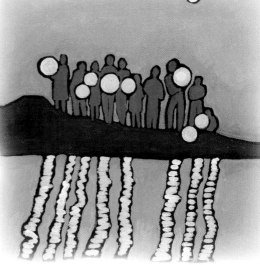

Glory to God in the highest,
and peace to his people on earth.
Lord God, heavenly King, almighty God and Father,
we worship you,
we give you thanks,
we praise you for your glory.

Lord Jesus Christ, only Son of the Father,
Lord God, Lamb of God,
you take away the sin of the world: have mercy on us;
you are seated at the right hand of the Father:
receive our prayer.

For you alone are the Holy One,
You alone are the Lord,
You alone are the Most High, Jesus Christ,
With the Holy Spirit,
In the glory of God the Father.

Amen.

Confirmation Prayer

Blessed are you, Lord our God.
Your glory fills the whole universe.
Wherever you are, there is brilliant light
that cannot be dimmed.

Blessed are you, Lord our God.
At the very beginning of all things,
you made light for our universe
and separated the light
from the darkness.

You gave us the sun,
a great glowing ball of fire,
to light up our days
and energize our whole world.

And at night when darkness covers the earth
the stars, the planets and the moon blaze in the sky,
guiding the lost and reminding us that you never forget us.

Blessed be God! O blessed be God!

Session 5

Awakened to Grace

Dear family,

At our gathering we recalled the final rite of baptism, when the Church prays that our ears will be opened to hear God and our lips opened to proclaim God's praise.

God's presence – grace – is a gift that permeates all creation and we must decide whether to embrace God's presence or ignore it. We need God's help to become aware of God's presence in our lives. The Holy Spirit helps us become aware of God in our lives.

During these final days before confirmation you are encouraged to continue to pray together.

- ✳ Read together and then talk about the questions on pages 41 and 42.
- ✳ Pray together the prayers on pages 43 and 44.
- ✳ Review together the outline of the rite of confirmation and share the information with the sponsor. (See the handout "How Is Confirmation Celebrated?")

We look forward to celebrating the sacrament of confirmation with you on

_____ at _____.

We will meet for our last session on _____ at _____.

Thank you.

Catechist

Growing in Faith

Because baptism marks the beginning of our journey as Christians, we recalled our baptism throughout our confirmation preparation. Confirmation completes baptism and both baptism and confirmation lead us to participate fully in the celebration of eucharist.

Sit quietly for a few minutes and recall the different rituals from our gatherings together. What do you remember from the water ritual? What did you discover about your baptism?

In Session 2 we used perfumed oil and praised God for the many wonderful gifts of creation. What message remains with you? On page 16 read once again about chrism, the oil used in confirmation.

Growing in Faith

The cross is a special symbol for Christians. It reminds us of our baptism and of our new identity as followers of Christ. What do you recall from Session 3 when we wore special clothing?

"You are the light of the world.... Let your light shine before others so they may see your good works and give glory to your Father in heaven." (Matthew 5:14, 16) How are you the light of the world? Look again at page 36 and ask the Holy Spirit to guide you to be light for others.

As disciples we gather to give praise and thanks to God each Sunday. We try to listen to the Holy Spirit so that we may see with the eyes of faith. Our journey as disciples is taking us down new paths together. How can your family continue to grow in faith?

Psalm 100

Make a joyful noise to the Lord, all the earth.

Worship the Lord with gladness;

come into his presence with singing.

Know that the Lord is God.

It is he that made us, and we are his,

we are his people, and the sheep of his pasture.

Enter his gates with thanksgiving,

and his courts with praise.

Give thanks to him, bless his name.

For the Lord is good;

his steadfast love endures forever,

and his faithfulness to all generations.

Breathe on me, Breath of God.

(adapted from the original text by Edwin Hatch)

Breathe on me, Breath of God,
fill me with life anew,
that I may love what you love,
and do what you would do.

Breathe on me, Breath of God,
until my heart is pure,
until I want whatever you want
to do and to endure.

Breathe on me, Breath of God,
dwell within my mind,
until every part of me
glows with fire divine.

Breathe on me, Breath of God,
so shall I never die;
but live with you the perfect life
of your eternity.

Session 6

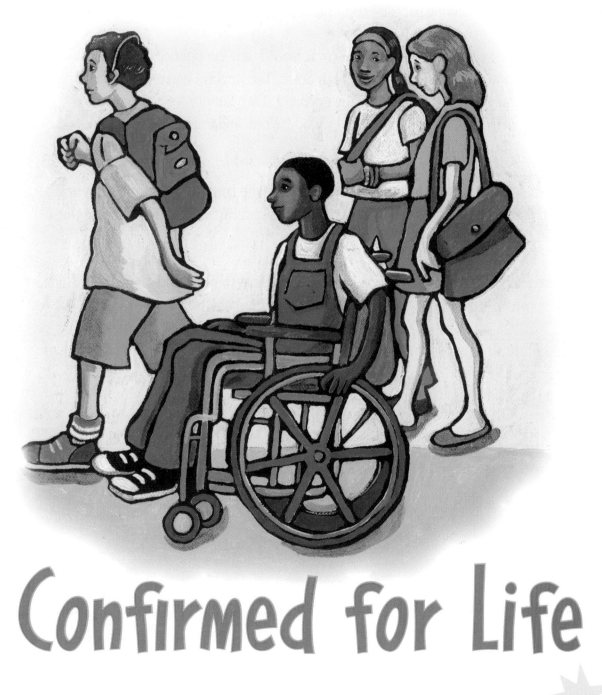

Confirmed for Life

Dear family,

At our final gathering we recalled the celebration of confirmation and focused on the strong connection among baptism, confirmation and eucharist.

In baptism we become a member of the royal, priestly and prophetic family of God. In confirmation we are anointed with the Holy Spirit. The weekly Sunday gathering of the Christian family is when we celebrate the eucharist. Each Sunday we give praise and thanks for all God's gifts, are nourished by God's Word, and share the body and blood of Christ at the table of the eucharist.

When the priest says, "Go in peace to love and serve the Lord," we leave the gathering to do the work of God, to be apostles. An apostle is sent by God to bring Christ to the world. Confirmed Christians are to be apostle-like.

You are encouraged to read the ideas on Bringing Christ to the World on page 47. Think of an apostolic activity your family might like to do. There is a list of ideas on page 48.

The confirmation preparation has ended and the work of living as a confirmed Christian now begins in earnest. Although our sessions have ended, we look forward to seeing you at the Sunday eucharist and in our parish life.

Thank you.

Catechist

Bringing Christ to the World

At the end of each eucharist we are told, "Go in peace to love and serve the Lord." We are sent with a purpose. We are to love and serve the Lord at home, school, in our parish and in the community.

There are many different ways that you and your family bring Christ to the world. Make a list of some things you are already doing. There are many other ways we can bring Christ to the world. Add some new ideas.

What We Already Do

....

....

....

What We Can Do in the Future

....

....

Apostolic Activities

We love and serve the Lord by loving and serving others. Sometimes we care for those we know. At other times we are called to care for people we do not know and may never even meet! When we care for others and serve them as Jesus taught us, we are doing apostolic work.

Your family may choose an apostolic activity to complete together. The following are just a few ideas of ways to bring the Christ to the world.

* Twice a year, clean out your clothes closet and take some clothing to an organization that assists others.
* Buy an extra Christmas present for a child and donate it to a children's agency.
* Volunteer to assist with a parish project.
* Make homemade treats and deliver them to a nursing home or retirement centre.
* Sponsor a child in a developing country.
* Become more involved in recycling and reducing the amount of waste.
* Help a neighbour with lawn work or shovelling snow and accept no payment.

As apostles we are called to co-operate with the Spirit of God so that the kingdom of God will flourish. This work is ongoing, so as we grow older we choose new apostolic work. Every Sunday when we gather for eucharist we are nourished, strengthened and sent forth into the world.